India Tibet Relations

(1947-1962)

India Tibet Relations

(1947-1962)

Claude Arpi

(Established 1870)

United Service Institution of India

New Delhi (India)

Vij Books India Pvt Ltd
New Delhi (India)

Published by

Vij Books India Pvt Ltd
(Publishers, Distributors & Importers)
2/19, Ansari Road
Delhi – 110 002
Phones: 91-11-43596460
Mob: 98110 94883
e-mail: contact@vijpublishing.com
web : www.vijbooks.in

First Published in India in 2023

ISBN: 978-93-89620-99-3

Contents

Introduction

The end of the 1940s saw momentous events which, in one way, redesigned the world.

Two years after the end of WWII, India got her Independence from the British; in October 1949, the sleeping Dragon, Communist China rose when its Great Helmsman announced the creation of the People's Republic of China from the rostrum on Tiananmen Square.

Mao Zedong was very quick to move. By the end of December 1949, with the blessings of Stalin, he had annexed Eastern Turkestan (today Xinjiang) and reached the gates of India, north of the state of Jammu & Kashmir.

In January 1950, Beijing announced its next step on the Asian chessboard; it would 'liberate' Tibet, Formosa (today Taiwan) and the Island of Hainan.

While the communists advanced their pawns towards India's borders, some leaders in India continued to imagine a perfect world and soon their main strategic objective became to avoid at any cost a world conflict.

It is with this background that the study of Tibet-India relations between 1947 and 1962, conducted under the Field Marshal KM Cariappa Chair of Excellence of the United Service Institution of India, witnessed the rise of the two Asian giants, with two different purposes, one could say, two opposite visions of the world - one wanted to dominate Asia with its foreign ideology, while the other dreamt of world peace.

Unfortunately in the process, India lost a century-old buffer zone between its Northern plains and the Middle Kingdom.

By the beginning of 1951, Tibet and Xinjiang were militarily absorbed into the new People's Republic of China. Many Indian political leaders soon realised that the *Hindi-Chini-Bhai-Bhai* honeymoon between Delhi and Beijing as envisaged by the Indian Prime Minister could only translate into the loss of a peaceful frontier for India.

Unfortunately, Sardar Vallabhbhai Patel, the Deputy Prime Minister and prime opponent of this policy, who presciently foresaw the implications for his country, passed away on 15 December, 1950, leaving Jawaharlal Nehru to freely continue his policy of 'friendship' at any cost, with consequences very much present more than 70 years later.

Paradoxically, the Indian officials posted on the Roof of the World quickly discovered the true objectives of the communists. But tragically, after Patel's death, nobody in Delhi or the Indian Embassy in Beijing was ready to listen to the intrepid officers.

This study goes in depth into the slow break-down of the age-old Indo-Tibet relations, gradually being replaced by a cruder relation with the new occupiers of Tibet. India's friendly relationship with its Buddhist neighbour was progressively terminated by the presence of the PLA on the plateau. During these fifteen years, not many Tibetans had the courage to fight the ineluctable; most of them, whether from the aristocracy or the clergy, collaborated with the occupying forces, particularly in the first years after the invasion.

The fifteen years under study witnessed a series of momentous events - starting with the annexation of Xinjiang and the closure of the Indian Consulate in Kashgar (end of 1949/1950), the invasion of Tibet (end of 1950), the signature of a 17-Point Agreement (May 1951) between China and Tibet, and the arrival of the Chinese troops in Lhasa (September 1951).

During the first years of occupation, the reports of the Indian Trade Agent in Yatung, Gyantse and Gartok, as well as of the Indian representatives in Lhasa, vividly described the changing trends in the power balance on the plateau. The Indian officials, who for decades dealt directly with the Tibetan authorities, had now to pass through the Chinese PLA officers.

China started to build strategic roads, most of them towards the Indian borders or worse, through Indian Territory in the Aksai Chin in Ladakh.

As the situation continued to deteriorate on the plateau, India and China decided to engage in the 'Tibet Talks' in Beijing (which started on 31 December, 1953). The negotiations, which culminated with the signature of the Panchsheel Agreement in April 1954, saw India losing all the rights it had in Tibet since the beginning of the 20th century.

This bi-lateral accord between Delhi and Beijing redefined India's age-old trade relations with Tibet; but the Tibetans themselves were excluded from the negotiations and the benefits of the Agreement.

In many ways, it marked the tail end of the events set into motion by the entry of Younghusband in Tibet in 1904. While the British expedition indicated recognition of Tibet as a separate entity (for the Western power), the signing of the Agreement put an end to Tibet as an independent nation.

The circle was closed, with incalculable consequences for the Himalayan region and India in general.

It took a few more years and many persistent Chinese intrusions on Indian soil to sensitise the Indian Government and public to the gravity of the new state of affairs.

The third and fourth parts of our study go further into the deteriorating situation on the Roof of the World, with Communist China tightening their grip on the administration, trade and religion. Despite a visit to India of the Dalai Lama and the Panchen Lama in 1956-57 for the 2500th Buddha Jayanti celebrations, the down-sliding could not be stopped.

This tense situation culminated in the events of March 1959, which saw an uprising of the Tibetan population in Lhasa and the flight of the Dalai Lama who took refuge in India.

Soon after, the border intrusions turned into armed clash on the frontier (Longju, Spangur Gap, etc.). This marked the beginning of the 'dispute' with China over the Northern boundaries of India.

The three following years saw the Chinese 'preparations' for the onslaught on the Indian borders. Our narrative finishes with the border war between the two Asian giants in October 1962, which shattered the Indian Prime Minister's dream of an eternal friendship with Communist China.

The Indian presence in Tibet ended with the lapse of the Panchsheel Agreement in April 1962 (it was not renewed) and the closure of the Consulate General of India in Lhasa in December 1962. This marked the end of an era.

The study has recorded in great detail these events which continue to have implications 60 years after the armed conflict in NEFA and Ladakh; the consequences can still be seen today in Eastern Ladakh and other sectors of the Tibet-India boundary, which has unfortunately become the Sino-Indian border.

Today, the Chinese propaganda would like us to believe that Tibet has always been part of China, but historical records show that it is not a fact and that the relations between Tibet and India are as ancient as the Himalayan ranges. Fifteen years have been documented through more than 2,000 pages. To put these facts on record was the main purpose of our study under the Field Marshal KM Cariappa Chair of Excellence.

Part 1

The Last Months of a Free Nation

The first volume (1947-1951) recounts the tragedy that befell Tibet; not only did the Dalai Lama and his people lose their country, which had lived blissfully ignorant of the great revolutions reshaping the rest of the world, but it became a tragedy for India too as it lost its peaceful neighbour, Tibet. Suddenly India had to share a border with Communist China whose ideology was the opposite of Buddhist values. At that time Delhi did not realise the importance but a few years later, when India would understand that it no longer had a secure northern border, it was too late.

Letters, cables, telegrams, and notes accessed by us showed that two schools of thought emerged during the tumultuous months of November/December 1950 - on one side were the then Prime Minister Jawaharlal Nehru and KM Panikkar, his ambassador in Beijing, both obsessed by an imaginary friendship with new China and fixated on the 'larger implications for World Peace'. The other school realised the strategic implications for India.

In a way, the fate of Tibet and India's borders with Tibet were sealed once Sardar Patel, who clearly foresaw and articulated the dangers of the Chinese annexation of Tibet for the Indian frontiers, passed away on 15 December 1950; hardly two months after the entry of the People's Liberation

Army (PLA) in eastern Tibet. Nehru's policy would have disastrous consequences which can still be felt today on the Indian borders, whether in Ladakh, Sikkim, or Arunachal Pradesh.

The Records in India

For decades, we have had to read the post-independence history of the Indian sub-continent based on primary sources from British, American, Russian and, sometimes, even Chinese archives. One cannot blame the historians who used these sources; still today, it is difficult to access the Indian archives, particularly the records of the Ministry of External Affairs.

Due to an old bureaucratic mindset, no declassification system has been put in place since independence. It is not that the declassification process is not governed by a law in India; legislation exists. All documents older than 25 years need to be declassified unless there is a serious security angle to prevent it. The Public Record Rules, 1997, state that records that are 25 years old or more must be preserved in the National Archives of India (NAI) and that no records can be destroyed without being recorded or reviewed.

Legally, it is mandatory for each ministry or department to prepare a half-yearly report on reviewing and weeding of records before submitting it to the NAI. The rules also stipulate that no public records which are more than 25 years old can be kept classified or destroyed by any agency unless it is properly appraised. Unfortunately, this is not done. As often in India, the law does not apply to the government which is above these human contingencies, though, in most cases, it is not in India's national interest to keep these old files closed to the researcher.

The refusal of the government to release the Henderson-Brooks-Bhagat Report on the 1962 Sino-Indian War is one well-known case. Another one is the 'Sikkim Papers' relating to the archives of the Gangtok office of the Political Officer (PO) who overviewed the Indian relations with Tibet, Sikkim, Bhutan and NEFA since Claude White, the first PO in 1890, till the merger of Sikkim in 1975.

These 'papers', though sent from Gangtok to Delhi under CRPF escort in 1976, are said to be 'lost'. It is a fact that no government official is today able to say where the priceless files have vanished. This author was one of the first to access the Jawaharlal Nehru collection, also known as the 'Nehru Papers', kept at the Nehru Memorial Museum Library. Though the collection only contains what passed through the first Prime Minister's Office, we were nevertheless able to decently reconstruct what happened in Tibet and on India's borders during the period under study.

To complement this study, we were able to obtain the few declassified reports sent from Tibet, available in the National Archives of India or other sources.

A Free and Independent Nation

What happened to Tibet during this crucial period (1947-1962) is a tragedy. There is no doubt that Tibet's system of governance had serious lacunas (particularly in the interregnum between the two Dalai Lamas), but the Land of Snows was free and independent. In October 1950, when Mao's regime entered Eastern Tibet to 'liberate' the country, 'liberate from what', was the question everybody asked.

Though at that time the Prime Minister did not realise it, it would soon be a disaster for India too, which suddenly had to live with a new neighbour whose ideology was the opposite of Buddhist values worshipped in Tibet.

The world, particularly the United Kingdom, which had regular diplomatic relations with Tibet for decades, decided to remain silent to avoid another Korean-type conflict. Only the tiny Costa Rica had the courage to take the Tibetan issue to the United Nations. More than seventy years later, the Tibetans still can't understand what happened to their country and why nobody asked them if they had wanted to be 'liberated' in the first place.

An Assessment of the Situation on the Roof of the World

Arthur Hopkinson, who entered the Indian Civil Service in 1920, took-over as Political Officer (PO) for Sikkim, Bhutan and Tibet in 1944. He continued in this post till India's Independence and like his colleague Hugh Richardson, who was the head of the Mission in Lhasa, he was asked by the Government of India to continue 'till Indian officers are able to take the frontiers' mantle.

On 1 August 1948, while visiting Yatung in the Chumbi Valley adjacent to Sikkim, Hopkinson wrote a secret 'review' of the situation in Tibet between August 1945 and August 1948 from his camp office.

He had to visit the Tibetan capital as "two abnormal difficulties necessitated a visit". One was a vacancy to head the now-Indian Mission at Lhasa; Richardson was soon reappointed by the Indian Government.

The other difficulty was a trade boycott, enforced since several months by the Tibetan Government. Hopkinson records that it was announced by the Lhasa Government in a truculent letter.

'Another outstandingly truculent' letter denounced the British trying to reassert their legitimacy over what Hopkinson calls, the Assam Tribal area (i.e. the McMahon Line area).

9

Tibet's Treaty with British India

According to the British officer, both communications meant a breach of treaty by the Tibetans, who had signed agreements with India in 1914 in Simla; Hopkinson said that it indicated 'an unfriendly Tibetan attitude'.

He however admitted that for the McMahon Line area "the Tibetans are justified only to the extent that we slept over the boundary provisions of the Simla Convention for nearly thirty years and no Tibetan, however highly placed, will ever undertake the onus of publicly acknowledging Indian ownership of territory hitherto regarded by them as Tibetan".

Referring to the Tawang area; the PO was keen to get a 'tacit acquiescence' of the 1914 Simla Convention: "[It] was the objective of my talks with leading individuals at Lhasa and ultimately, of the memorandum presented in January 1946; we insisted on the validity of the Treaty Line inviting them to specify what alterations (if any) they wanted in that line".

Hopkinson's two-month stay in Lhasa in 1945-46, bore its fruits and "backed by steady onward pressure and firmness on the Assam side, we succeeded in securing this objective of tacit acquiescence".

This is not exactly true, as during the next two years the issue would continue to haunt the relations between India and Tibet. But "thanks to official steadiness and tact, Tibetan opposition became increasingly negligible," wrote the PO, who admitted, "While in Lhasa the matter was never again seriously raised for nearly two years, when circumstances attending the Transfer of Power seemed to give the Tibetans another opportunity of once more raising this old favourite".

However, in 1948, "the new effort does not appear prima facie to be very convincing".

The PO was unhappy when during war-time, the Tibetan government attributed the trade difficulties "to the perversity of the Government of India [...] and the Political Officer in particular". A senior Tibetan Cabinet minister once sarcastically asked: "Do European hens lay fewer eggs during the War?"

The British were aware of the importance of business to regulate bilateral relations. During his visit in 1935, Sir Basil Gould had promised to do everything to facilitate bilateral trade.

In 1948, Hopkinson affirmed, "We have deliberately set out to demonstrate to Tibetans the economic and commercial advantages of the connection with India, in order that, when changes should come, the economic and commercial bonds should hold firm, preserving the Indian connection intact against all other stress and strains".

The Tibetan accusations against the PO were not really fair.

Poor Communications with Tibet

However, noted the PO: "We have, properly speaking, no road link with India; for our truck road is interrupted by a bridge (the Rambi bridge) which vehicles [cannot cross] - its renovation has been annually postponed since 1943; while the sole rail communication, the Darjeeling Hill (D.H.) small gauge railway between Giellekhola and Siliguri, long ago ceased to be able to cope with the traffic".

The Tibetans did not appreciate these difficulties; they believed that the mighty British Empire could do miracles [...]if it decided so.

The Chinese, when they marched into Tibet in the early 1950s, would act decisively and take actions on a war-footing;

11

they immediately started building roads (including the Qinghai-Tibet and the Sichuan-Tibet highways inaugurated in 1954) as well as the Aksai Chin road (through Indian Territory) which would be completed in July 1957.

"But there is another side to the medal", wrote Hopkinson, "It is common knowledge that every Tibetan is at heart a trader: the commercial instinct is no creation of ours".

The PO commented that during the War and immediately after, "the facilities for easy and cheap procurement provided by the control system, the high prices offered by China and later by Nepal accelerated the tempo and created a get-rich-quick atmosphere that tended to debauch and demoralize Tibetans (not all Tibetans) of all classes".

It had a demoralising effect and "someone who would never have dreamt of doing so before, now sticks out the hand and uses the word 'buckshish', a word previously unknown". It is also true that the largesse of the PO's Office toward some Tibetans certainly did not help to make Tibet a responsible State.

Good Manners Endangered?

Despite these 'difficulties', Tibetan manners were outstanding, noted the PO. There is little crime even among the Tibetan muleteers at Kalimpong, "Muleteers are nowhere Saints, but a collection of Tibetan mulemen at Kalimpong would compare well with a corresponding collection of say, Powindas at Jamrud".

Hopkinson compared the Tibetans to the Pathans of the North-West Frontiers: "without being showy or swash-bucklers like the Pathans, they are just as virile and muscular [. ....]They are not prepared to stand nonsense, but without being aggressive, offensive or vindictive. They have

12

knives and they like a gamble, but they do not, like Pathans, conclude their gambling parties with a stab in the belly". He then concluded, "Tibetans are above all friendly and cheerful. [...] They sing invariably at their work, the labourer, the mason, the ploughman, in all the field operations, the lonely shepherd-boy on some wind-swept mountain-side and all sing tunefully".

Hopkinson's report provides a good description of the situation in Tibet at the time of India's Independence. Hopkinson mentioned the story of the English school which was opened in Tibet, before he took over from Basil Gould in Gangtok in 1944. It was the second time in twenty years that a school was opened at the Tibetan behest. The first was in Gyantse, this time it was in Lhasa. Both the times it had been "almost immediately closed in deference, it was said, to conservative prejudice against such a disturbing element".

Ironically one of the Tibetans responsible for the closure was a high official who had sent his own son to a European school in Darjeeling. Later the same official also sent another of his children to India for schooling.

The Problem of the Minority

A far more serious issue was that "no individual in Lhasa is willing to undertake responsibility or take a lead, it is difficult to find where plenary power lies". Even the Chinese representative complained to the PO about the issue of the 'Minority'. Hopkinson had realised this when he first visited Lhasa in 1945 to discuss the McMahon Line with the Tibetan authorities.

Three years later, he noted: "Doubtless as the result of a long minority regime, Tibet has for several years had a government weak and for the most part ineffective, ignorant and perplexed amid the changes and chances of this wicked world, composed for the most part of individuals interested in their own personal profit, but at the same time patriotically anxious to preserve Tibet's special status: apt to seek defence in procrastination, in temporisation and obscurity of language". Ultimately this cost Tibet its independence.

A Tibetan Newspaper

The PO was however impressed by *The Melong*, the first Tibetan language newspaper published from Kalimpong by Tharchin Babu, a missionary originally from Kinnaur. The PO believed that: "help and encouragement [from the Indian Government] is desirable. ...Now promoted from a broken-down litho-machine to a regular printing press, this paper has progressed greatly, not without effort applied from without. It has proved its popularity and usefulness, which further effort and patience will develop greater potential usefulness; not the least, it discourages hostile journalistic efforts".

The Thirteenth Dalai Lama was said to be a subscriber of the publication in the early 1930s.

Tibet Political Isolation

On the political level, Tibetan efforts to contact the 'outside' world were 'pathetic'. According to Hopkinson: "owing partly to inexperience, partly to carelessness in the choice of representatives, partly to neglect in the important matter of interpreters".

The PO observed that the Chinese would accept nothing short of complete Tibetan surrender: "Nor likewise has the change of regime in India induced them to tone down their claims on Indian Territory in Assam".

Hopkinson concluded that Communist or Nationalist rulers have the same irredentist attitude.

The PO quoted Charles Bell who had predicted that after India got Independence, "Tibet might move away from Indian into a closer federal relationship with China and during the period before the transfer of power the report was [that] Independent India intended to 'sell out' to Chinese imperialism over Tibet".

India's Presence in Tibet

The establishment in Tibet consisted of the Indian Mission in Lhasa, the Indian Trade Agencies in Gyantse, Yatung and Gartok, and the military escort to which the ITA in Gyantse and Yatung were entitled.

In June 1947, the haste with which the British Government decided to divest themselves of their responsibilities in India caused the Tibetans to wonder whether they were about to be deprived of the diplomatic support enjoyed so far under the British Raj. The Tibetans themselves did not really understand what was happening.

The first communication of the Government of Independent India to the Foreign Office of the Tibetan Government was to request the latter to ratify current bilateral treaties, particularly the Simla Convention. This formal request from the Government of India to the Foreign Office of Tibet was itself a proof of Tibet's independent status in 1947.

The Tibetans would eventually take nearly a year to answer the communication: "The delay was unfortunate, as also the lack of clarity at that time in respect of the continued legal validity of the treaties".

Retrospectively, it certainly cost Tibet its independence. It was a first blunder.

Hopkinson remarked that eventually, "commonsense prevailed not without extraneous aids". He added: "some important individuals had practical reason to realise the implications of the lesson, Tibetan dependence in economic and commercial matters on India," before concluding, "Tibet has now given the requisite assurances. The hesitations and uncertainties of 1947 are now, happily, of the past. Tibet does indeed want to reciprocate India's friendly feelings: and all appears set fair for the future of Indo-Tibetan relations".

The situation would soon get more complicated, with the entry of a new player, Communist China.

Indian Military Escort in Tibet

According to a note prepared by the Historical Division of the Ministry of External Affairs in the 1950s, the posting of an armed escort at Yatung trade mart was first discussed in connection with the opening of the trade mart in Tibet under the terms of the 'Regulations regarding Trade, Communication and Pasturage of 1893', appended to the Sikkim-Tibet Convention of 1890.

After the desirability of providing an escort to the officer posted at Yatung to supervise the Indo-Tibetan trade was examined, it was implemented.

The historical note explained the scruples of the British rulers: "Later on, however, in order to avoid any ill-feeling or suspicion of Tibetans even the officer who went to Yatung to attend to the details connected with the opening of the mart was not allowed to take an escort and had to be satisfied with an escort provided by the Chinese representatives".

At the time of independence, the escorts still existed. It would be the subject of discussions during the talks for the 1954 Tibet Agreement.

KM Panikkar in Nationalist China

On 22 November 1948, KM Panikkar, the Indian Ambassador to China posted in Nanjing, wrote a top secret note addressed to the Prime Minister about the happenings in China and the arrival of the Communists. The note was tellingly entitled, 'When China goes Communist'. Panikkar began by a description of the evolving situation in the Middle Kingdom. By the end of 1948, it was clear that the time of the Nationalists was over and it was only a matter of months for Mao to come to the helm.

Interestingly, the officer who two years later would be one of the main advisors for the Tibet policy and would offer the Roof of the World to China on a platter, was still lucid.

The Secret Visit of Major ZC Bakshi to Tibet

Soon after Independence, the Government of India, though not ready to get involved in a full-fledged military operation in Tibet, was still studying different options.

In the summer of 1949, in order to have a proper assessment, the Minister of External Affairs decided to send a young Army officer to survey the eventual routes, which could be used to send troops and ammunition in the event of a 'political' decision to defend Tibet. The officer was also asked to check on the military preparedness of the Tibetan Army.

The fact that this covert mission took place and this with the knowledge of KPS Menon, the Foreign Secretary, is proof that in the summer of 1949, the Government of India was still keeping all its options open.

1950: The Year of the Iron-Tiger

In mid-October, Chamdo, the capital of Kham Province was captured and when the PLA reached the junction of the

Lhasa road, the retreat of the remaining Tibetan troops was blocked. Ngabo, the Governor of Kham capitulated without fighting on 17 October and ordered the Tibetan army to surrender to the Chinese troops.

A month later in Lhasa, Tenzin Gyatso, the young Dalai Lama was invested with the temporal power during a ceremony attended by the Indian, Nepalese and Chinese representatives in the Potala Palace. The Oracle had repeatedly advised the Tibetan Government to confer full power to the fifteen year old boy. When asked again, he said: "Make Him King".

On 24 November an appeal of the Tibetan Government was taken by the General Committee of the UN. India intervened to request the UN to keep the matter pending and assured the world body that they would find an amicable solution between the Tibetans and the Chinese. Sixty five years later the matter is still pending!

On 15 December, Sardar Patel passed away. India lost a great leader with a clear vision and a strong will. In a letter to the Indian Prime Minister written a month earlier (drafted by Sir Girja Shankar Bajpai), he had clearly pointed out the folly of trying to appease the Chinese at any cost. In loosing Patel, Tibet also lost a friend and a supporter.

The death of Patel was the turning point in the Tibet policy of the Government of India. From now on nobody could stand up to Nehru; a policy of vagueness and appeasement would prevail, till it was too late. The Sardar however had started the ball rolling on the borders by creating a Defence Border Committee which ordered the take-over of the administration of Tawang less than two months later.

In December 1950, the debate in the Indian Parliament showed the ambivalence of Nehru's position. While the

Indian Prime Minister admitted in the Parliament[1] that it was not clear from whom China wished to liberate Tibet, but at the same time he also declared that he "attached a great importance to India and China being friends".

The following years would show that he was more interested in the friendship of China than the defence of India's borders and the fate of Tibet.

On 21 December, the Dalai Lama left Lhasa for Yatung Valley to take refuge near the Indian border where he thought he could eventually begin some negotiation with the Chinese on the future status of Tibet. Although some people criticised his move to leave Lhasa, history had taught the Tibetans that the only chance (if there was still any) to negotiate with the Chinese was to be out of their hands.

By December 1950, the game was over; the outcome was already written and the sequence of events for India, Tibet and China had only to slowly unfold itself.

The Takeover of Tawang Administration

India needed to avoid the blunder of Kashmir where large parts of Indian Territory was literally 'offered' to a hostile neighbour. Fortunately, some officers were determined to safeguard India's interests. Tawang found its own 'Patel' in Jairamdas Daulatram, the Governor of Assam.

In early January 1951, Daulatram orders a young Naga officer to go and set up the Government of India's administration in Tawang area (then known as Kameng Frontier Agency).

Till the end of 1950, the entire area from Tawang to Dirang Dzong, south of the Sela Pass, though part of the Indian Territory, was still under some vague Tibetan

---

1   On December 6, 1950.

19

administration, with the Tibetan *dzongpon* of Tsona in Tibet, collecting 'monastic' taxes from time to time in and around Tawang.

It is here that Major Bob Khathing of the Assam Rifles entered the scene. Accompanied by a couple of hundred troops of the Assam Rifles, Bob Khathing finally reached Tawang on 7 February 1951.

An excellent article written by Yambem Laba in the *Imphal Free Press* quoted the Naga officer: "[...] two days were spent scouting the area for a permanent site where both civil and military lines could be laid out with sufficient area for a playground. A place was chosen north-east of Tawang Monastery and a meeting with Tibetan officials was scheduled for 9 February, but they had shown a reluctance to accept Indian authority overnight".

The journalist remembered Khathing telling him in 1985 (he had accompanied Khathing on his last trip to Tawang) that he had no option, but to order Captain Limbu to ask his troops to fix the bayonets and stage a flag march around Tawang "to show he [Khathing] means business".

Apparently, it had the desired effect and in the evening the Tibetan officials and elders of the monastery came to meet the Political Officer. They were told that from now on the Tsona *dzongpons* or any representatives of the Tibetan Government would no longer exercise any power south of Bumla.

Strategic Thinkers vs 'Visionaries'

A first observation about the period 1947-1951: India had some of the best strategic thinkers, but the government did not use their competence; their conclusions were not accepted by Prime Minister Nehru. These farsighted Indian thinkers deserve the homage that they have still not yet received.

Two factions emerged during the tumultuous last six months of 1950- one obsessed by an imaginary friendship with New China. The other, which immediately saw the strategic implications for India, if Delhi let Tibet down, was led by Sardar Patel, the Deputy Prime Minster with Sir Girja Shankar Bajpai, the Secretary General of the Ministry of External Affairs and Commonwealth Relations as his main adviser. They were fed by reports 'from the ground' by Harishwar Dayal, the Political Officer in Sikkim and Sumal Sinha, the Head of the Indian Mission in Lhasa. At that time, India had a full-fledged Mission in Tibet as well as three Trade Agencies in Gyantse, Yatung and Gartok.

The 'Chinese' Ambassador Panikkar had opposite views. In one of his lengthy reports, Panikkar explained to Nehru, "Tibet is now in the process of being 'liberated'. The word 'liberation' (*Chieh fang*), it may be made clear, does not in Chinese signify a military conquest. It means the introduction of new life and the elimination of misery, moral degradation, inequality of sexes, etc., in fact liberation from the oppression of tradition. The 'liberation' of Tibet is, therefore, being attempted mainly through education and propaganda".

More than seventy years later, the Tibetans have still not experienced the 'education' aspect of the the 'liberation', which the Ambassador was so enthusiastic about.

Who were the 'Visionaries'?

Sardar Patel, who so presciently articulated the dangers of the Chinese invasion for India's frontiers, passed away on 15 December 1950. Thereafter, Nehru's line prevailed unhappiness, with disastrous consequences.

A personal letter written by Harishwar Dayal the PO to Maj SM Krishnatri, then posted as the Indian Trade Agent

(ITA) in Gyantse, is telling. While discussing the Chinese advance towards the McMahon Line, the PO informed the ITA of Sardar Patel's death, "It is a heavy blow. He was the one person in this Government who had strong realistic view of things, including on foreign relations. Now, we are left at the mercy of the visionaries".

It was truly the case.

The Korean Conflict

An important factor in our story was the role that India wanted to play in the Korean conflict. It greatly influenced Delhi's Tibet policy. By January 1951, the Ministry of External Affairs and the Indian Embassy in Beijing had started to spend most of their time and energy on 'peace-making'; in the process; Tibet was abandoned.

In fact, by the beginning of 1951, the 'Tibetan incident' was over for the Indian Ambassador in China. India could start dreaming of an eternal friendship with China. In the Annual Report of the Indian Embassy for 1950, Panikkar wrote, "The exchange of notes on Tibet, following the Chinese attack on Chamdo gave a temporary setback to our relations, but the reaction of the Chinese Government to the Indian protests was restrained and neither country permitted this incident to have more than a temporary effect. India consistently supported Chinese claims in the United Nations and her sustained efforts to settle the Korean issue have been fully appreciated in China. There is every reason to hope that the next year will see even better relations established between the two countries".

But India had lost a peaceful border, a friendly neighbour and instead acquired a belligerent one.

The Three Phases

If one analyses the events, the first period of this research could be divided into three phases.

➢ Phase 1: August 1947- September 1949

➢ Phase 2: October 1949- August 1950

➢ Phase 3: September 1950 – May 1951

During the first two phases, the policy of the Government of India towards Tibet remained as it had been during the British period.

Through Phase 1, life on the Roof of the World continued as in the past several decades. The Dalai Lama was growing into a bright adolescent and nobody bothered much about the revolutions happening in the world[...]and the decolonisation.

Nehru's government had reappointed two Britishers to their jobs: Arthur Hopkinson, who had served as the last British Political Officer in Sikkim (Hopkinson continued to officiate till mid 1948) and Hugh Richardson, as the head of the Mission in Lhasa. Both played an important supporting role with their great clarity of mind; they understood the importance to maintain relations with Tibet 'on the old basis', and more particularly, they realised the implications for India of an eventual Chinese 'adventure' on the plateau.

It must be noted that their successors Harishwar Dayal and Sumul Sinha would be treated very differently by the Indian Prime Minister than the British officers. Had Richardson received from Nehru one of the reprimands that Sinha received a few months later, he would have immediately returned to his native Scotland. But Sinha had no 'island' to leave for; after his tenure in Lhasa, he was a broken man.

July 1949 saw the pre-emptive expulsion of all Chinese living in the Tibetan capital. But all that was to change on 1 October 1949 when the Communists took over the Middle Kingdom.

Independent India primarily sought to maintain a kind of status quo, i.e. Tibet continuing to be a buffer between China and India, while trade and religious exchanges through the Indian borders flourished. By June 1948, Lhasa had accepted the past treaties and conventions between British India and Tibet, but there were no efforts to delineate, demarcate and secure the northern boundary as Buddhist Tibet was a friendly neighbour. All was well!

The second phase (from 1 October, 1949 till August 1950) was marked by the emergence of an irredentist New China. The relations between India and Tibet however remained unchanged even when the Communist propaganda started announcing the 'liberation' of Tibet. Very few in Delhi took it seriously. What was the Indian Intelligence doing? Did they ever read the speeches or declarations of the Chinese leaders? They probably thought it was mere propaganda for the internal audience. It was not. India clearly failed to evolve a strategy or at least a pragmatic policy, to deal with Communist China, Further, leaders such as KM Panikkar or VK Krishna Menon thought that the arrival of Mao on the stage was the best thing which could have happened to China [...] and Tibet.

The third phase started with the military operations in Tibet. It was officially announced by a letter of Marshal Liu Bocheng which was dismissed by the 'visionaries'; around the same time (August 1950), Panikkar changed 'suzerainty' into 'sovereignty', giving a green card to Communist China to invade (or 'liberate' in Red jargon) Tibet. Indian policy during this period was marked by accommodation and unbridled appeasement towards China.

The strategic interests of India were sacrificed on the altar of 'wider world views' or perhaps the fear of jeopardising the chances of the Peoples Republic of China (PRC) gaining entry into the United Nations Security Council.

From the western powers' point of view, as mentioned by a US diplomat, the main concern was "let us not rock the boat", as in any case, "it is India's business".

It is striking to follow the utter pragmatism behind the decisions taken by Mao Zedong and his colleagues as compared to the Indian foggy philosophical concept of 'world peace', which only led to immense sufferings for the Tibetans and India. One can only hope that lessons will be drawn from this?

Part 2

Will Tibet Ever Find Her Soul Again?

The second volume (1951-1954) looked at the consequences of the signing of the 17-Point Agreement in May 195. The Tibetan delegates had no alternative but to accept that "the Tibetan people shall return to the family of the Motherland of the People's Republic of China" and "drive out imperialist aggressive forces from Tibet".

A two-phase operation had been meticulously planned by Mao Zedong - the first part culminated in the Battle of Chamdo which saw the Tibetan forces being decimated. The Great Helmsman's second step was 'diplomatic', the weak Tibetan State was forced to put its thumb impression on an agreement allowing Communist China to take over the Land of Snows. This period also saw the beginning of the Hindi-Chini-Bhai-Bhai honeymoon between Delhi and Beijing.

This ended with the signing of the 1954 Tibet Agreement to which the Tibetans were not even invited to participate. For the Indian negotiators, India's long border with Tibet (now China) was wishfully deemed 'settled' in the process, while the Chinese would wait to raise the issue at the 'appropriate time'.

The Aftermath of the 17-Point Agreement

The Tibetan had further agreed that "The local government of Tibet shall actively assist the People's Liberation Army

(PLA) to enter Tibet and consolidate the national defenses". (Article II)

As the *Hindi-Chini-Bhai-Bhai* honeymoon between Delhi and Beijing had started, very few realised then that this could only be against India. Over the next months and years, the Indian officials posted on the Roof of the World would discover the true attitude and objectives of the Communists; but nobody in Delhi or the Indian Embassy in Beijing was ready to listen, resulting in the deterioration of the age-old Indo-Tibet relations, gradually being replaced by a cruder relation with the new occupiers of Tibet.

This period ended on 29 April 1954 in Beijing, with the signature of the "Agreement on Trade and Intercourse between the *Tibet* region of China and India" by the Indian Ambassador N. Raghavan and Zhang Hanfu, the Chinese Deputy Foreign Minister; because of its preamble, it is today referred as the *Panchsheel Agreement*.

The years between 1951 and 1954 were marked by a general worsening of the situation in Central Tibet and the slow take-over of the institutions by the PLA and the representatives of the Central Committee of the Communist Party of China (CCP). It seemed ineluctable after the signature of the 17-Point Agreement and Delhi's surrender of India's interests in Tibet for the sake of a mythic friendship with China. The Head of the Indian Mission in Lhasa was the first to realise that Tibet would never be the same.

The Situation on the Ground

During the years following the 17-Point Agreement, India's friendly relationship with its Buddhist neighbour progressively disappeared under the pressure of the Chinese administration and the presence of the PLA on the plateau. Very few Tibetans had the courage to fight the ineluctable;

most Tibetans, whether from the aristocracy or the clergy, collaborated (at first) with the occupying forces. At the same time and paradoxically, the early 1950s saw the birth of a national conscience and a 'people's movement', which unfortunately never got Delhi's support.

The Chinese troops arrived in Lhasa in September 1951, preceded by General Zhang Jingwu, the representative of the CCP's Central Committee.

The meeting of Sumul Sinha, the head of the Indian Mission in Lhasa with the Chinese General is fascinating in the sense that the subsequent happenings could already be perceived in this 'polite' encounter.

During the first year of occupation, a report of the Indian Trade Agent in Gyantse vividly described the changing trends in the power-balance on the plateau. The Indian officials, who for decades dealt directly with the Tibetan authorities, had now to go through the Chinese PLA officers.

The Indian Prisoners of War

An issue which has never been narrated before is the fate of the four Indian prisoners of war during the 'Liberation War', i.e. the invasion of Tibet in the summer of 1950. After several months of hard negotiations, four young Indian radio operators were finally freed. The Indian diplomacy did a good job in that particular case.

These youngsters from the Himalayan region who had been employed by Robert Ford, a British man working as a radio operator for the Tibetan Government, were accused of trying to obstruct the 'Liberation of Tibet'. Retrospectively, the illegal detention of the young radio operators was shocking.

Feeding the Enemy

One of the strangest episodes is the 'feeding' of the PLA by the Indian Government, who allowed large quantities of rice to transit via its Territory for more than two years to feed the starving PLA.

Without Delhi's active support, the Chinese troops would not have been able to survive in Tibet. Cables, telegrams and despatches between Lhasa, Yatung, Gangtok, Delhi and Beijing enlighten us on this weird happening.

What lessons could be learnt from the episode? Clearly India's ostrich-like attitude towards China's occupation of Tibet cost her heavily and it is advisable not to feed the army of a potential enemy, especially when this army is busy constructing road to your borders. The cost of strengthening the PLA's presence on the plateau would soon be obvious.

The Administration of Tawang

The situation in Lhasa and elsewhere in Tibet continued to deteriorate, the strengthening of the Indian borders was imperative. For the purpose, an Indian Frontier Administrative Service was created and several ex-Army officers were recruited. This was one of the positive outcomes of the new tensions on the borders. These remarkable officers performed miracles on the frontiers.

While the Chinese were pushing their administration forward in Western and Southern Tibet, the Indian Government was slowly advancing towards the McMahon line. The administration of Tawang was in good hands, thanks to Maj Bob Khathing and his colleagues, though the difficulties were immense.

Maj Khathing managed to smoothly run the Tawang administration and effectively protected the local Monpa population against the rapacious Tibetan tax collectors' exactions.

In 1951, the North and Northeastern Border Committee, led by Maj Gen Himmatsinghji, the Deputy Defence Minister, had suggested providing basic amenities and a proper administration to the tribal population living south of the McMahon Line in NEFA's five Frontier Divisions; this was done in difficult conditions, mainly due to the inhospitable terrain and sometimes unfriendly tribes.

The Indian Frontier Administrative Service played a crucial role in this context. The remarkable service, with outstanding officers, more or less at par then with the Indian Administrative Service, greatly helped consolidate the Indian borders in the North-East in the early 1950s.

While the NEFA on Tibet's borders started witnessing quick developments, it has to be noted that during the early 1950s, China never claimed Tawang or the entire NEFA; today, Beijing terms the whole area 'Southern Tibet'.

The Closure of the Indian Consulate in Kashgar

When one looks at the fate of the Tibetan nation, the closure of the Indian Mission in Lhasa and its renaming as a Consulate General, thereafter working under the Indian Embassy in Beijing, is yet another tragedy never recorded in India's history books. Delhi accepted it meekly, without even informing the Parliament that India 'officially' had a new neighbour.

Another tragic event took place at the same time - the closure of the Indian Consulate General in Kashgar.

Both events would have long-term implications for India, it can be seen even today, seventy years later. Delhi no longer has a representation in Tibet and Xinjiang. The *de facto* closure of the Indian Consulate in Kashgar in Xinjiang in 1950 implied that the customary trade between Kashmir and Central Asia, via Ladakh and Xinjiang came to an end. The famous old Silk Road was dead.

In the present days, the reopening of any new Silk Road has no meaning if these regions are unable to have contacts with India. Delhi may have to take a stand on the issue one day, if it wants to participate in the Belt and Road Initiative (BRI) sponsored by Chinese. Without these traditional outposts, how could India play a meaningful role in the region?

The Traditional Trade

Another fascinating aspect rarely mentioned in history books is the flourishing trade with the Himalayan States of Tehri-Garwal, Himachal Pradesh as well as Ladakh through the seasonal Indian Trade Agency in Gartok, one of the three agencies functioning under the office of the Political Officer (PO) in Sikkim. The trade with Tibet in the Western Himalaya has been documented by Lakshman Singh Jangpangi, the ITA in Western Tibet. For years, he represented the Indian Government in these desolate areas; his diary is a treasure recording a world which does not exist anymore.

The flourishing business in Yatung located at the gate of Sikkim in the Chumbi Valley, also needs to be mentioned.

China soon started building strategic roads to Lhasa (the Sichuan-Tibet and Qinghai-Tibet highways) but also one through the Aksai Chin in Ladakh. Some Indian documents give an idea of the Chinese troops' deployment in the early years of the Chinese occupation.

Very few Indian politicians realised at that time the importance of developing the border areas as a way to counter Chinese advances (and propaganda).

31

Minsar Principality

While the Indian administration continued to advance in the NEFA, India also had a presence in Western Tibet in Minsar, an Indian village, located near Mount Kailash, which was traditionally a part of the J&K State.

This would soon be forgotten for the sake of the nascent friendship with the Communist regime, but the legal facts remain unchanged. Seventy years later, even if Minsar is still part of Indian Territory, it is today difficult to enforce the possession of the village (as it was in the 1950s).

As a result of the rapid decrease of the trade in Western Tibet, the Himalayan regions slowly lost their main sources of revenue, which translates even today in a migration out of the border villages.

Over the first few years of the occupation of the plateau, one can see the situation slowly changing with the Chinese getting bolder and establishing themselves by force, imposing their law on the local Tibetan officials as well as the Indian representatives. The pilgrims to Mt Kailash and the traders from the Himalayan region and Ladakh started to face more and more harassment.

Delhi seemed to close its eyes to the tragedy happening in the high Himalaya, as more important 'world' issues had probably to be tackled.

The Tibetan at a Loss

The Tibetans were at a loss, should they collaborate with the Communists or revolt against the Chinese occupation? Interestingly, it was the poorer sections of the society which would start to rebel, while the high clergy and the aristocracy was not unhappy with the Chinese largesse.

In Lhasa, Gyantse or Shigatse, many Tibetans happily collaborated with Chinese; they could not grasp the implications of their 'liberation' for the future of the Tibetan nation.

The tide continued to turn against the Tibetans during the following years. The Indian representatives in Tibet could do little to change this course of events; it was the time when Delhi was increasingly enamoured with Communist China.

Consolidation of the Chinese Presence

While these momentous events were taking place on India's borders, the PLA military consolidation on the Tibetan plateau continued at a fast pace.

What is most surprising is the fact that India was very much aware of the details, but the political leadership read China's intention totally wrongly.

The lesson is that an ideological viewpoint can hamper an accurate geostrategic vision of a situation, and ultimately have disastrous consequences for the nation. Accurate information was available, but the leadership closed their eyes.

A bunch of notes from the CIA on the infrastructure development in Tibet, as well as the Indian recce on the Chinese military deployment, give frightening insight on the Chinese intentions in Tibet and Xinjiang. It was the time when the Aksai Chin road linking the two 'liberated' provinces started being built.

Delhi 'Unaware' of the Dangers looming over the border

In Delhi, very few officers had the courage to call a spade, a spade. Sumul Sinha, who had previously been posted as the Head of the Indian Mission in Lhasa, was one of them. Now serving in the North-East Division of the Ministry of External

33

Affairs, he dared to mention in a note, 'The Chinese threats on the NEFA'. He would be blasted by Prime Minister Nehru, who still relied on KM Panikkar, now Indian Ambassador in Cairo, to advise him about India's China policy. Sumul Sinha was a dejected officer, though some ten years later; his reports appeared to have been prophetic.

One of the saddest aspects of these years, is the Indian leadership's total lack of understanding of the 'Chinese Threat'.

The Tibet Talks

Finally, at the end of 1953, negotiations started for a new agreement with Tibet. The consequences of China's occupation of Tibet, were to be settled in a couple of weeks; it would take four months to arrive at a settlement …but leaving out the border in the process (Zhou Enlai had said on the first day that only issues 'ripe for settlement' would be solved, but nobody understood what he meant). Slowly over the weeks and months, India would give away all its rights in Tibet, but getting nothing in return.

Further, the fact that the Prime Minister wanted 'quick results' did not help. The Chinese negotiators extracted concessions one after another; in many cases, it was plain unnecessary surrender of the Indian diplomats.

At the end of the 'talks', Delhi discovered that the main Indian negotiator dealing with the Chinese, a married man, had a Chinese girl friend who he wanted to marry; he would have to be replaced by the Indian ambassador. It was a tragic moment for the Indian diplomacy, though the lapses have never been acknowledged by the Indian side.

The 'Tibet Talks', in which Tibet never participated (was not even informed), ended after four months with the signature of the Panchsheel Agreement.

The signing of this bi-lateral accord between India and China redefined India's age-old trade relations with Tibet; the Tibetans themselves were excluded from both the negotiations and the benefits of the Agreement.

In many ways it marked the tail end of the events set into motion by the entry of Col Younghusband in Tibet. While the British expedition indicated recognition of Tibet as a separate entity, the signing of the Agreement put an end to Tibet as an independent nation. The circle was closed, with incalculable consequences for the Himalayan region and India. The other misfortune is that the Agreement would be remembered not for its content, which triggered the slow destruction of a 2,000 year-old 'way of life', but for its preamble (the Five Principles) which was supposed to govern the relations between India and China.

Prime Minister Nehru based India's relation with China, on his *Hindi-Chini Bhai-Bhai* policy, but the idealistic Principles would never be followed either in letter or in spirit, by the Communist China.

It took a few more years and many persistent Chinese intrusions on Indian soil to sensitise the Indian Government and public to the gravity of the situation.

For several years, Nehru naively believed his Chinese counterpart when Zhou Enlai told him that the world would be changed "when Panchsheel would shine over the universe like a sun".

Tail End

The devastating floods in Gyantse in July 1954 washed away the building of the Indian Agency and several Indian officials, including the ITA, and the Officer Commanding-designate (OC) of the military escort, would lose their lives; a tragic and symbolically ominous end to a distressing period of turbulent changes. China would never allow the Agency to be rebuilt despite the Agreement.

Part 3

Tibet: When the Gods Spoke

The Years after the Panchsheel

It is a fact that the Dalai Lama had been quite impressed by the changes he had seen during his visit to China in 1954-55 and he certainly had no objection to seeing new communication links being built in Tibet. The zeal, efficiency and dedication of new China's leadership had made an impression on the young Dalai Lama and some of his colleagues. Many of these qualities were missing in the large monasteries of Tibet at that time.

In some ways, after the signature of the 'Panchsheel' Agreement, India lent an open support to the forces which led to the complete loss of a 'way of life', based on the eternal values shared with Indian culture.

By accepting to put an official seal on the Communist takeover of the Roof of the World, India not only condemned to certain death an old civilisation with its imperfections and its realisations, but made herself somewhat complicit, through her acceptance, to a philosophy of violence and brute force.

After having masterfully secured the Indian withdrawal from Tibet through the 1954 Agreement, the Chinese consolidated their presence on the plateau. This is the object of the third volume (1954-1957).

A major consequence of the Panchsheel Agreement was the advance of the Communist ideology on the Tibetan plateau. A new way of life, less compassionate, less enlightened, slowly took over the Roof of the World.

India's withdrawal from Tibet and the happenings on the plateau left Tibet's small neighbours, Sikkim and Bhutan, deeply worried; in 1956, the first revolts took place in Kham province.

These momentous events as well as the creation of the Preparatory Committee of the Tibetan Autonomous Region, which was to bring new 'reforms', started to be resisted by the Tibetan masses.

The visit of the Dalai Lama and the Panchen Lama to India in 1956-57 on the occasion of 2500th anniversary of the birth of the Buddha is an important event. What is striking is that at no point in time were the Tibetan Lamas involved or even consulted in the acceptance of the invitations.

Eventually, the two Lamas returned to their homeland, to give the Communists a 'last chance' to respect their promises.

The PO's Views on the Situation

Apa Pant, the 'philosopher' Political Officer in Sikkim was dealing with Tibet in the Ministry of External Affairs; Pant visited Tibet in 1957 and sent a long report to Delhi.

Though he was aware of the strategic importance of the Tibetan plateau, Pant was often more interested in the humane aspects. The government's romantic approach led to the loss of a peaceful border.

Pant wrote, "With all its shortcomings and discomforts, its inefficiencies and unconquered physical dangers, here was a civilisation with at least the intention of maintaining a pattern of life in which the individual could achieve liberation. Without the material conveniences that others have come to expect, the Tibetan as I found him was a cultured, highly developed, intelligent person whose vision, supported by the constant example of the monastic order, was fixed upon the objective of reaching Nirvana. It was a perspective that must make a Tibetan pause and think before accepting communist solutions as the right and only ones for the problems of an ancient society on its way into the modern age".[2]

Pant readily admitted that he always felt "a great admiration for China's culture and civilisation, for its long history and indeed for its new revolution".

However, he was saddened by the Chinese incapacity to accept (or even understand) a philosophy not fitting in with the Party line. This was, he believed, the main reason for the failure in the relations between China and the Dalai Lama. But this analysis also shows a lack of understanding of Mao's thought process.[3]

Chinese officials in Tibet, like Gen Zhang Jingwu, did not look favorably at the Dalai Lama's aspiration to radically change the Tibetan society, while also maintaining 2,000-year old traditions, for the simple reason that it could have cast a shadow on the rule by the Communist Party.

Pant like many of his colleagues, felt that the Tibetans had a lot to learn from the Chinese, "In my travels in Tibet I observed how disciplined the Chinese were. All their

---

2   Pant Apa, *Mandala - An Awakening* (New Delhi: Orient Longman Limited, 1978), p. 112

3   See Volume 1, Chapter 8.

activities were directed towards the building of a new culture, a society of new men".

This proved to be a myth; though Pant was already regretful: "The Chinese could have remedied this warped [social] aspect of [Tibetan] society by helping the Dalai Lama to institute social, political and economic reforms, which he was most eager to do... young as he was, in the hope of Chinese cooperation in a 'modernizing' programme, while retaining what was good and valuable"[4].

In the course of his visit to Tibet, Apa Pant had the occasion to discuss these points with the Chinese generals, who could only answer in terms of Marxism and Party discipline; the so-called reforms had then just started.

It is a fact that once the Tibet Agreement was signed in April 1954, the Chinese leadership took a more radical approach towards Tibet, though, for a couple of years, the main factor which determined this approach was the building of the infrastructure needed to 'stabilise the revolution' on the plateau.

Pant felt that the Chinese officers were not interested "in harmony and compassion but in power and material benefit"; it was an occasion for Pant to philosophically ponder upon the confrontation of these two different worlds, "The one so apparently inefficient, so human and even timid, yet kind and compassionate and aspiring to something more gloriously satisfying in human life; the other determined and effective, ruthless, power-hungry and finally intolerant. I wondered how this conflict could resolve itself, and what India's place in it was".[5]

---

4   Pant, op. cit., p. 114.

5   Ibid, p. 115.

This last sentence sums up the deeper ramifications of the survival of Tibet as a separate nation. Was it possible to preserve and develop these human qualities in a new Tibet? The future would show that it would not be.

The Lama Hierarchy and 'Modern' Tibet

It is true that most of the senior Indian diplomats, educated in 'modern' ideas, thought the 'old Lama hierarchy' should go and Tibet become a 'modern' country. They believed that the Chinese invasion was a chance to make a clean sweep of the old superstitions, beliefs or rituals. The Indian border was forgotten in the process.

Pant commented, "In those corridors of power [South Block], it often appeared, Tibet, Buddhism, the Dalai Lama, were all regarded as ridiculous, too funny for words; useless illusions that would logically cease to exist soon, thanks to the Chinese, and good riddance".[6]

Pant had some support in the Ministry of External Affairs for his 'philosophical' approach, but few could comprehend the strategic and military aspect of the events unfolding on the Roof of the World.

The First Intrusions

Paradoxically or ironically, this very period witnessed the first Chinese intrusions in Barahoti, a small flat grazing ground located in today's Chamoli district of Uttarakhand. Though the first two of the Five Principles spoke of 'Mutual respect for each other's territorial integrity and sovereignty and Mutual non-aggression', the Chinese troops walked into the Indian Territory before the ink on the treaty had dried.

---

6   Ibid.

41

During the following years, many such intrusions took place in the Central Sector of the Indo-Tibet border, which had become the Sino-Indian border.

On the diplomatic front, the process began with Premier Zhou Enlai's visit to Delhi in June 1954 and followed by Jawaharlal Nehru's trip to Beijing in October, to culminate a year later in the Bandung Conference. Hardly any words about Tibet were exchanged during the encounters between Nehru and Zhou; for the Indian and Chinese leaderships, it was a settled issue [...] except for the border. The Tibetans were nowhere in the picture.

At that time, the Indian Government started noticing some cartographical aggression by Beijing, the details of Delhi's handling of the issue and the 'misunderstanding' about what Beijing called 'old maps' would continue during the following years.

India Relinquishes her Rights in Tibet

In Tibet itself, it was time for India to wind-up her presence on the plateau. The negotiations took many more months than expected, particularly for the *dak*-bungalows. But in early 1955, an agreement would be finally found. A few photos show the extent to which some of these guest houses were really valuable buildings, but the political decision had been taken to simply hand them over to China. A similar fate awaited the military escorts in Gyantse and Yatung; in a rather discreet manner, it was soon withdrawn. Delhi was probably ashamed to have even a scarce military presence in Tibet.

The Road Construction in Tibet

With the passing months, the consolidation of the Chinese presence in Tibet continued, it translated into the construction of several roads leading to Lhasa. The two main axes (Tibet-

42

Sichuan and Tibet-Qinghai) reached the Tibetan capital in December 1954. This adversely affected the bilateral trade, suddenly, the PLA no longer needed Indian grain and other commodities.

Whether the Chinese leadership had made up its mind about implementing the 'reforms' in Tibet or not, their first strategic objective was clear, they needed to construct the infrastructure across the plateau on a war footing, as these roads lead towards the Indian border.

By 1955, the construction of the Tibet-Sinking Highway (today's G219) cutting across Ladakh (Aksai Chin) had started and the roads leading towards the NEFA (now Arunachal Pradesh) and Sikkim had already been completed.

Zhou's words were definitely linked to the development of the communication infrastructure when he proclaimed that the Tibetan society was 'not yet ripe' for socialist changes.

Pant believed that Nehru understood the depth of the conflict; however "the exigencies of power, the feeling that the Chinese must in no circumstances be 'upset' and the needless, nervous and desperate hurry to 'normalize' India-China relations, lost us the larger perspective of action".

These are some of the factors which contributed to the rapid disappearance of one of the planet's most ancient civilisations; it was to be replaced by a more materialistic culture.

Hope against Hope

Pant was quite clear about the outcome of the situation, the Tibetans were hoping against hope. They did not have the assurance that they would get the benefits brought by the Chinese on the material plane, while maintaining "the old system and the philosophy that taught and practised the path towards liberation of the human mind from turmoil".

Development in the North-East

While watching the development taking place on the Tibetan plateau, the the Roof of the Worls's tiny neighbours, Sikkim and Bhutan were deeply worried about their own future.

Delhi had to work out new policies for these States, as well as for her own border areas. The visit of India's Foreign Secretary RK Nehru to Sikkim, Tibet (Chumbi Valley) and Bhutan was an important event in this new political context.

While the changes in NEFA, particularly in Subansiri and Tawang Frontiers were vital, the leadership in Delhi did not understand the strategic issues triggered by the occupation of the Tibetan plateau for her borderlands. It translated into, for example, sending the anthropologist Verrier Elwin on a mission to Tawang, which, though interesting in itself, neglected the military and strategic aspects which were systematically overlooked by the Indian State. It would have disastrous consequences a few years later, though intrepid officers such as Maj SM Krishnatry and Capt Sailo clearly described the 'imperiled' border of India.

On the other side of the plateau, in Western Tibet, life continued as usual; Indian traders continued for sometime to carry their goods from the Himalayan region and while the Chinese presence was still at a minimum, the PLA focused mainly on building new roads. However, the attention of the Communists was brought by the Tibetans, to the borders areas such as Barahoti or Nilang Valley. This would have long-term consequences for India; the Chinese intrusions still happen today every summer.

The visit to China of Kushok Bakula Rinpoche of Ladakh was an important event which unfortunately did not make the Chinese reconsider their policies or make the

Indian Government realise that something was going wrong in Tibet.

The First Revolts in Eastern Tibet

It was also the time of the first uprisings in Kham province of Eastern Tibet, the 1956 revolt was followed by a violent repression by the Chinese Army. Though not directly related to India Tibet relations, this momentous event as well as the creation of the Preparatory Committee of the Tibetan Autonomous Region, which was to bring new 'reforms', often unwanted, to the Tibetan 'masses' are worth noting.

Incidentally, it is the Tibetan 'masses' known as *Mimang*, the People's Association, which revolted first against the occupation of their land, while the clergy and many aristocrats accepted the new situation, for their own interests.

The Indian Government could only be a silent spectator to the happenings triggered by the signature of the two agreements (the 17-Point Agreement with the Tibetan representatives in 1951 and the so-called Panchsheel Agreement signed with India three years later), both legalised the Chinese presence on the plateau.

The Tibetan Lamas' visit to India

The visit of the Dalai Lama and the Panchen Lama to India on the occasion of 2500th anniversary of the birth of the Buddha was an important event. What is striking is that at no point in time were the Tibetan Lamas involved in the acceptance of the invitations.

At the last minute, in December 1956, after months of reluctance, Beijing agreed to the visit. It was a risk for Beijing, which knew that many Tibetans were keen that the Dalai Lama should take refuge in India. The Chinese Premier Zhou Enlai visited Delhi thrice in less than three months between

45

November 1956 and January 1957; he wanted to make sure that the Tibetan leader would return to Tibet. In the process, Zhou promised to postpone the Communist 'reforms' for a few years.

Eventually, the two Lamas returned to their homeland, to give a 'last chance' to the Communists to respect their promises.

Could India have played a more proactive role? However, for many Indian officials, reforms were necessary and the Chinese presence was not entirely a bad thing for Tibet. In the process, they forgot to take into account the impact of the Chinese occupation of the plateau for the Indian border.

Another Lesson

One lesson to be drawn from the events of this period is that philosophy is not enough to guard the borders of a nation.

Mao Zedong had declared, "The philosophers have so far only interpreted the world, the point is to change it"; without adopting the concept of 'power flows from the barrel of the gun', the defence of a nation's borders cannot be neglected, at the peril of serious consequences, as was witnessed five years later.

The visit of Tawang by an anthropologist is telling in this perspective; the total neglect of the defence preparedness of the borders for the sake of a romantic theory is something which should never happen again.

During these years, India not only lost a good neighbour, which for centuries had deep cultural, economic and emotional exchanges with the subcontinent, but also a secure border.

Looking at the visit of the Dalai Lama and the Panchen Lama to India, one realises that India and Tibet no longer had a one-to-one relationship, for every important decision or even small details, they had to deal through a third party, the Communist China. The case of their invitation is illustrative.

At the same time, the Chinese were rather nervous about the situation developing in Eastern Tibet. This probably explains why Zhou Enlai had to visit India thrice during the two-month stay of the Lamas in India. The Chinese Premier had to make sure that the Dalai Lama returned to the Land of Snows; this was not a good omen for the future.

Part 4

The End of an Era: India Exits Tibet

The Most Dramatic Period

The fourth and the last part of this research deals with the period 1957-1962 which witnessed the most dramatic events of the bilateral relations between India and Tibet. The consolidation of China's military presence on the plateau, followed by the uprising of the Tibetan masses in March 1959, prompted the Dalai Lama to flee to India, where the Tibetan leader and tens of thousands of his followers became refugees. Though the Chinese propaganda projected the March 1959 events as the 'emancipation of the serfs', the reality was very different.

The reports from the Indian Trade Agents in Gartok, Gyantse and Yatung, as well as the Consul General of India in Lhasa give glimpses of a disappearing world; an era was coming to an end.

Mao's China did not want any Indian presence in 'their' new colony. A sense of suspicion and envy towards India prevailed. Beijing clearly resented the existence of an age-old civilisational relation between India and Tibet.

By 1959, the relations of the Indian Consul General and the Trade Agents were no longer with the Tibetan Administration of the Dalai Lama, even in the months before the departure of the Tibetan leader for India, but solely with the Chinese authorities, most of them senior officials of the Peoples' Liberation Army (PLA).

At the government level, the relations between the People's Republic of China and India had taken a turn for the worse, particularly after the Tibetan rebellion of March 1959.

The last Indian Consul General, Arvind Deo admitted that when someone has served in Lhasa in these prevailing circumstances, any other diplomatic posting was unproblematic. One can presume that this was true for all other officers who served in Gyantse, Yatung or the remote and inhospitable Gartok in Western Tibet.

The period ended with a war, an outcome which should have been expected when one looks at how the situation on the ground in Tibet was developing and the deteriorating relations between the new bosses on the plateau and the Indian representatives in Tibet. One can only be full of admiration for the Indian officials posted on the Roof of the World, they served their country well, trying valiantly to maintain a decent relationship with the occupiers.

The Writing on the Wall

It is sad that the leadership in India did not see the tragedy unfolding, slowly but surely.

The 1957 visit of Pant, and the short stay of the Indian Prime Minister at Yatung in the Chumbi Valley on his way to Bhutan and back in September 1958, should have been eye-openers for Delhi. It was not to be, though retrospectively, through the account of the Political Officer , one realises that the situation had already gone beyond anybody's control and there was no question of Five Principles of peaceful coexistence with China any longer.

But, Delhi continued to dream, probably not knowing what else it could do, it could not open its eyes to the ground reality.

One is struck by the aggressiveness of the Communist regime, its capacity to call white what was black and to accuse India or its representatives of non-existent wrongdoings.

The Communist Party was able to justify its ruthless presence on the plateau only through intense propaganda. Why did the Indian leadership not see through the bluff and anticipate the tragic outcome?

It is not as though all the required information was not available, the reports of the successive Consul Generals, most of them brilliant and courageous officers, faithfully gave detailed accounts of the increasing difficulties with the new rulers. But, India was still hoping and dreaming of a great, if not eternal, friendship between India and China.

On the ground, each and every line of the reports of the Indian Trade Agents makes it clear that the Communist Party did not want an Indian presence on the plateau. Interestingly, one of the Indian officials remarked that there was a jealousy factor. Tibet had always been (and still is) closer to India, whether spiritually, culturally, politically or simply at the human level. Communist China has always (and still does today) resented this fact.

The Turning Point

The events of March 1959 were the main turning point. First, for the Chinese, the Tibetan rebellion was the best opportunity (and exercise) to prepare for the War of October 1962. Most Chinese accounts admit this today. The PLA learnt a lot from the fight against the Khampas, particularly in terms of logistics, joint operations and acclimatisation on the plateau.

Second, once the Dalai Lama was out of his native country, there was no restraint shown anymore by Mao Zedong's ruthless regime to impose the so-called reforms on the recalcitrant Tibetans.

A firsthand account of the Tibetan uprising of March 1959 sent by Maj SL Chibber, the Indian Consul General in Lhasa contradicts completely the Chinese version that Beijing helped the serfs to liberate themselves from the yoke of the feudal landlords. The 1959 Uprising was a popular mass movement. The Chinese propaganda may continue to propagate its false narrative, but Chibber's account will also remain to tell the truth of the revolt.

Whether Mao let the Dalai Lama leave Lhasa or he realised too late that the Tibetan leader had left his Palace on 17 March 1959, is irrelevant; once the Tibetan leader safely reached India, the bridges were burnt, and soon after, the border became 'disputed', with incidents in Longju in NEFA and Kongka-la in Ladakh taking place, making India suddenly realise that the boundary was not settled, as had been wishfully thought by Delhi.

The hundreds of letters and notes exchanged between the two countries (and published in the 14 White Papers), bear witness to this.

Today the boundary dispute is the direct consequence of the Tibetan government in Lhasa losing its autonomy and its capacity to deal with its own frontiers. The centuries-old Indo-Tibet border became a Sino-Indian one, with the consequences that we can still see today.

The Rehabilitation

The Dalai Lama started a new life in India and a new type of relation evolved after tens of thousands of Tibetans followed their leader into exile. Nehru, during his first encounter with the Dalai Lama in Mussoorie in May 1959, made it clear that India would not politically support Tibet, but Delhi would help to rehabilitate the refugees and provide education to the youth. The Tibetan leader was probably shaken by this first meeting, but what choice did he have but to accept Nehru's decision?

In Tibet, the situation quickly worsened as we can see from the 1960 reports of the Consul General and the ITAs and once the Dalai Lama was given refugee status in India, the relations reached a point of non-return.

Looking at the diplomatic scene during these years, one realises that the Tibetans had no more say in the happenings on their own borders. The first attempt to solve the border issue between India and China was made in June 1958, when talks on Barahoti (Central Sector) were held in Delhi.

Not only did it lead nowhere, but China never kept its promise to refrain from sending armed patrols in the remote high-altitude plain of Chamoli district, it was another in a series of broken promises (after the 1951 Seventeen-Point Agreement and the 1954 Tibet 'Panchsheel' accord).

The Aksai Chin road was another issue which should have opened the Indian leadership's eyes about what was in stock for the Himalayan borders.

The Border Talks

In 1960, during the talks between the officials of the two countries, (which resulted in two separate Reports), the gap in perceptions of both countries appeared unbridgeable. It is not necessary to go into these issues which have been well-covered by many authors.

The 1961 boundary talks between Ambassador G. Parthasarathy and Zhang Wenji, a Chinese official, held in

Beijing were perhaps a last chance to peacefully sort out the issue. Ultimately no progress was made, politically, the views were too far apart. An assessment of the three encounters between the Indian and Chinese diplomats help to understand why the issue is still alive today.

The reports of Indian officials in 1960, the Consulate General in Lhasa or the Trade Agencies, demonstrated that the old relationship was coming to an end. Looking at the declining trade between Tibet and the Indian Himalayas (important for the survival of the border populations in India), the pilgrimage to Mt Kailash and Manasarovar or the fate of the *Kachis*, the Kashmiri traders in Tibet, the Communists made it clear that they did not want the Indian presence on the plateau.

The End of the Panchsheel

The logical end was that the 1954 Tibet Agreement, lapsing in June 1962, was not renewed, as Delhi thought that there was no point in continuing under those painful conditions. For example, the ITA in Gartok was still living every season in a tent; the Chinese did not allow, in spite of an agreement, India to build a proper agency building-cum-residence in Western Tibet, the situation was similar in Gyantse where the Indian ITA and his staff were living in deplorable conditions after the Agency was destroyed by the floods of July 1954.

In these circumstances, it became clear that there was no point to renew the 1954 Panchsheel Agreement and the Trade Agencies in Yatung, Gyantse and Gartok had to ultimately be closed; it happened in the spring of 1962.

The two years before the closure of the Indian diplomatic missions, saw a constant harassment of the Indian diplomatic personnel in Tibet who had to deal with thorny issues such as the fate of the Indian traders, the vicissitude of the pilgrims to

Mt Kailash, the status of the Kashmiri Muslims, in Lhasa or the nationality of the Ladakhi monks studying in the Tibetan monasteries.

Military Preparations

Military assessment reports, the details the PLA deployment on the plateau did not alert Delhi, as sycophancy had crept in around the powers-that-be in the years preceding the War, with incompetent politicians, intelligence and army officers coming to occupy important posts.

The appointment of Lt Gen BM Kaul as the Chief of General Staff after the retirement of General Thimayya as the Chief of Army Staff being one case in point. In the end, it resulted in a complete failure of the State which lost its capacity to estimate the waves of Chinese troops which would descend the slopes of the Thagla ridge in NEFA or in Ladakh in October 1962.

The reading of the White Papers on China makes all this clear. The PLA's preparations for a war were evident, except for Delhi living in its own world. The reports from Lhasa should at least have opened the eyes of the Indian intelligence agencies, it was not to be the case.

Another tragedy was the closure of the Indian Consulate in Lhasa around mid-December 1962, three weeks after the unilateral declaration of ceasefire by the Chinese.

During all these events, a sense of inexorability prevailed. Our story ends with a couple of not-too-well known aspects of the 1962 China-India War, in particular, the five-year 'training' of the PLA during the Tibetan insurgency, which greatly helped the Chinese forces become familiar with the terrain and other logistic difficulties on the plateau.

The POWs in Tibet

The fate of the PoWs kept in Tibet, reveals another tragedy within the greater tragedy which was the 1962 War.

Many documents of this period are still not declassified and it is difficult to reconstitute what happened in the last few months before the War with China. Why, for example, was the Indian Consul General in Lhasa called for consultations in Delhi as the War was starting? Why was the Consulate in Lhasa closed in mid-December 1962, even after China had declared a unilateral ceasefire on 21 November and hostilities on ground were almost over within a week or so?

This study ends with new findings on what happened to the 3,900 Indian PoWs in Tibet. It sheds some light on the seemingly uninterested attitude of the Government of India, who thrived on adhocism. One realises that after the October/November 1962 debacle, very few officers would have had the courage to take necessary decisions to preserve India's interests.

Retrospectively, one can certainly regret the closure of the Indian Consulate in Lhasa, a few words would be said about the unsuccessful attempts to reopen it in the 2000s.

The personal experience of a senior Indian officer who spent some six months in a PoW camp in Tibet is telling. The officer recounted, "After we were allowed to sit on top of our house in the sun, we would often see an old lama in the monastery above and if he caught our eye, he would take out his hand from under his robes for a split second and make a sign of blessings, as it were. After a few times we felt convinced that he was conveying goodwill to us. So, we would also make a quick sign of salutation with folded hands in return. He would never stay long in our sight".

The narrative continues, "One day, towards the end of our stay, at our request we were taken to see the palace and the monastery. It was a shock to see the palace with all the beautiful Buddha statues of all sizes and fabulous scrolls (*thankas*) lying broken, defiled and torn and trampled on the ground. In the monastery, a couple of lamas were still staying including the one we 'knew' by sight. When we were walking through the usual dark corridors on the conducted tour, this lama was just ahead of me with a guard in front. He sought my hand in the darkness and pressed it. I quickly responded with both my hands. This episode is mentioned just to illustrate the true feelings of Tibetans towards us Indians".

When Beijing speaks of reopening Old Silk Roads, it should be reminded that the roads between India and Tibet were based on centuries of kinship and shared values. No doubt, China has been able to annex Tibet by force of arms, whether they are able to assimilate Tibetans into their system is a moot question, the answer to which only the future holds.